I0472936

The Point Guard Entrepreneur

John E. Jones Jr

DENVER, COLORADO

Outskirts Press, Inc.
http://www.outskirtspress.com

ISBN: 978-1-4787-4847-2

Outskirts Press and the "OP" logo are trademarks belonging to Outskirts Press, Inc.

PRINTED IN THE UNITED STATES OF AMERICA

Table of Contents

Introduction

Limitless Success

What does "success" mean for an entrepreneur?

Entrepreneurs and employees have different definitions of success. As an employee, your success is defined by who you work for. Success is whatever you can fit between nine and five, Monday through Friday, while you're following the rules of someone else's dream.

But as an entrepreneur, your success is totally defined by you. When you are an entrepreneur, you have freedom. You dream your own dream, and you draw your own finish line. You have the power to create your life exactly the way you want it to look. For an entrepreneur, success has no ceiling.

For an entrepreneur, success is limitless.

My Path to Entrepreneurship

I've been in business for more than twenty-five years. I was the first African American to hold a position in the top 1 percent of independent contractors for a Fortune 500 company. I now own five companies of my own.

I've achieved my personal definition of success, and I live my life the way I feel it was meant to be enjoyed.

But I wasn't born into success. I grew up in a lower-middle-class family. Two months before I graduated from high school, I lost my father, and that made it very hard for me to go to college. I had to help my mother with my younger siblings.

I realized early on that a nine-to-five job wasn't for me. So I built my path to entrepreneurship from the ground up, using the principles I'm about to share with you.

You can build that path, too. To do it, you've got to become a point guard entrepreneur.

The Point Guard Entrepreneur

A point guard is the key player on a basketball team.

The point guard is like the coach on the court while the game is in motion. He gets the ball to the right people at the right time. He controls the plays. He directs the offense.

The point guard in basketball knows the vision of the coach. He knows the direction the team needs to go. He knows the players that he's surrounded by, how the play is designed to run, and how to redirect it when it gets off track. He understands the strengths of his team, and more than that, he understands the strengths of his opponents.

As an entrepreneur, you have to be the point guard for your business. You have to know your vision. You have to have the right players on your team so you can execute your plan. You have to be able to put those players in the right positions, and you have to be able to adjust when you make mistakes. On top of all that, you have to understand your competition.

You are the person in your company who designs the plays and leads your team to success. And believe it, you can survive. More than that, you can thrive.

The Game Plan

My goal with this book is to give you a game plan that will lead you to success as an entrepreneur. The game plan takes you through the five key plays of a point guard entrepreneur: dream, plan, have a strong work ethic, be willing to fail, and build a strong support system.

Understand that a game plan is not a master plan. It's a blueprint to get you started. As you move forward, you're going to come back to the five key plays in this game plan and build on them. You'll be able to use them to grade yourself. "How am I doing with my work ethic?" you'll ask. "What do I need to change in my support system?" Or, "You know what? I've slacked off on my organization. When was the last time I looked at my plan?"

The five key plays are areas of opportunity. Follow them when you open up your business. And two years, five years, or ten years down the road, come back to them again and ask yourself: "Wait a minute; am I still on track with my five key plays?"

That's how a point guard entrepreneur builds long-term success.

Tear Down Your Biggest Obstacle

Too many would-be entrepreneurs never get off the ground. They don't have enough money. They don't have enough time. They don't have enough experience. What they do have is a whole lot of excuses standing in their way.

They point the finger at every problem except the only one that really matters: themselves.

The number one factor when it comes to succeeding as an entrepreneur is you. You have to know how and when to start, and where you want your team to end up. Who calls the plays? You do. You're the first one in and the last one out of the office every single day. It's up to you to try new ideas on for size and to keep like-minded people around you who are as committed to success as you are.

As a point guard entrepreneur, you have to believe in your dream. You have to set the plan. You're going to have to work hard and be willing to fail. And you have to create a strong support system that will push you to succeed.

Following the five key plays of this game plan will give you the confidence you need to believe in yourself. When you believe in yourself, you overcome the hurdles in your way. And if your belief in yourself is strong enough, you have what it takes to succeed.

You have what it takes to be a point guard entrepreneur.

CHAPTER 1

Dream

The People's Talent Show

A friend and business partner of mine, Albert Gates, used to install cable for a living. He was tight with his money. He never spent anything at all. If someone wanted to go out to eat, he'd say "Let's cook something here." If we went out for drinks, he ordered water. One day, I asked him why.

It turned out that this young man watched all the singing and talent shows on TV, and he had a dream. His dream was not to be on one of those shows. His dream was to *create* one of those shows in his home city.

He dreamed of giving away TVs and iPads to his audience. He wanted to give $10,000 cash to one person in the audience, every show. The winners on the show would get $5,000. The school that brought the most students to the event would get $1,000. Each show would cost him between $25,000 and $30,000.

Before he turned thirty, Albert made his dream a reality. He called it *The People's Talent Show*. When he saw the first show go live, Albert had tears in his eyes. And the first check he wrote, he kissed it. He handed it to the lady who'd won, and he said, "Thank you."

"No, thank you," she replied.

Albert looked straight at her and said, "No ma'am, no ma'am. Thank you."

Albert never borrowed a dime from the bank. The day *The People's Talent Show* launched, newspapers came out to report on it. Nobody could believe that this young man had enough money to pull it off. But he did it. He did it because he followed his dream.

Dream Your Reality

Merriam Webster defines a "dream" as "a strongly desired goal or purpose."

Albert's talent show was his dream. Your dream is your personal reason for getting up in the morning. There are heartaches to being an entrepreneur. But those heartaches fall far, far short of the glory, the wealth, and everything else that comes along with your personal vision of success.

Your dream gives you the energy and motivation you need to push through every obstacle in your path.

Without a dream, a goal, or a purpose, you end up lost. No dream, no drive. People open up businesses every day, and many of those businesses fail within five years. You know why? Because those businesses weren't dreams. They were just thoughts. Maybe you can cook well. Maybe that's a skill you have. But that doesn't mean you're chomping at the bit to open up your own restaurant.

You have skills, and you have a dream. Know the difference, and follow your dream to success, because your skills alone don't provide the battery power to get you there.

The Point Guard Entrepreneur: Carry the Dream

In basketball, the point guard keeps the dream alive for his team. He keeps it in view of his players. He reflects back to it. When someone starts to lose energy, he pulls that player aside and reminds him how valuable he is—how he fits into the dream. Everybody on the team becomes part of the dream, because he pulls them into it and keeps them focused on the goal.

As a point guard entrepreneur, it's your job to bring your team into your dream just like that point guard on the basketball court.

The point guard can't win the game by himself. And you can't get the success you want without the creativity and energy of a great team behind you. As an entrepreneur, you don't have all the answers. That's why you have to pull your team into the dream. You have to keep your people focused on what you're all trying to achieve. And you have to let them contribute their ideas to your original vision.

Share your dream with your team, and let them help you build your dream even bigger.

When your people help you build the dream, that dream becomes real for them. They gain ownership in the business, and in turn, they want to see it succeed. They start caring about the results as much as you do.

When your people jump on board and start giving you ideas for your dream, your personal strength goes sky high too, because now you have a group that believes in what you believe in. Use that strength to motivate your team to keep pushing toward success. Even when the clock is ticking down those final minutes, it's up to you to have the drive to keep your people in the game.

You're a point guard entrepreneur, and you carry the dream.

Five Points to Dream for Success

Point #1: Make sure it's your dream. Your dream is something that you are willing to sacrifice everything for. If you're working for someone else's dream, you won't make the necessary sacrifices, and you won't succeed.

Point #2: Share your dream. The more you share your dream, the more people will join your dream, and the stronger your dream will become.

Point #3: Block out naysayers. If someone is giving you advice on how to get your dream started, great. But if they're telling you, "You can't open up a hamburger place because there are a million of them already," wipe that negative comment away.

Point #4: Write your dream down. Write down your dream, and then keep it in a place where you can see it every day. Post it everywhere to remind yourself what you're working for.

Point #5: Be your own point guard. Direct, oversee, call timeouts, and make changes for yourself as well as for your team. The stronger you are personally, the more your dream will thrive.

CHAPTER 2

Plan

The Road to Number 1

When I became the regional director in a brand new area of growth for a Fortune 500 company, I had one objective: to make my team number one.

The catch was that I didn't have a team to start with—not a single person. I had to hire independent contractors to work on a commission basis. Up front, they wouldn't get a dime.

I knew I wasn't going to get to number one by accident. I needed a plan. Before I even moved into my office, I wrote down how many people I needed, and what I needed each person to do. I built in space and contingencies for failure, knowing that something, somewhere, was bound to not work. I wrote down how often I was going to pull these people together to make sure the plan was still on track.

I planned the work. Then I worked the plan. I hired doctors, lawyers, everybody I could get to come work for me. I built a team from zero to over one hundred people in less than a year. I made adjustments when I had to, and I kept my team focused on the goal.

At the end of the year, we were the number one team in the organization. The success was incredible. And we had the plan to thank for it.

Plan to Succeed

Your plan is your roadmap as an entrepreneur. You need it to stay on track. When you get off track—as everyone does from time to time—use your plan to get you back to where you're supposed to be.

You draw your energy and your motivation from your dream. But if you don't have a place to direct all that energy, it spreads out everywhere, and you never get anything done. Your plan shows you where to direct the energy that comes from your dream.

Your plan guides you down the road to success.

Without a good plan in place, you will want to give up when things go wrong. It's inevitable that problems will come up in your business. If you haven't set down your intentions, ideas, and strategies for success ahead of time, then when those problems appear, you'll feel like you can't handle them. Without a plan, when you use up all your energy, you have no blueprint to rebuild it with. Reading your plan reminds you, "Oh yeah, that's right! This is what I want to do."

Your dream keeps you motivated to keep moving forward. But your plan keeps your focus on track for success.

The Point Guard Entrepreneur: Lead with a Plan

A basketball point guard is the coach on the floor. He shows his team how to execute the game plan because he leads by example. Then when he sees a player breaking from the plan, he has the credibility to pull that teammate aside. He reminds that player what the plan is and gets him back on track. Then he puts him back in the game.

A lot of entrepreneurs start out as one-person companies. So in the beginning, who are the players you're talking to? You're talking to yourself. Sometimes you have to sit yourself down and say, "Hey, today I didn't make the fifty calls I should've made. Am I following the plan? I have to keep on track. I have to do these things."

As your company grows, you have to lead your team with the plan, too. You use your plan to make sure that all of your people are on track and playing their part in what needs to get done.

Your plan is important, but it can't be set in stone. If you're not flexible with your plan, your business will drown. You won't be able to adapt to overcome obstacles.

So stay flexible. Stay with the plan. That's how you lead yourself and your team as a point guard entrepreneur.

Five Points to Plan for Success

Point #1: Meet with your team two or three times a month. Touch base with your people often to make sure that everyone is on track with the plan.

Point #2: Write the plan in pencil, not pen. Be flexible with your plan. Obstacles will come up in your business. If you plan to be flexible, you plan to succeed.

Point #3: Make the plan realistic. Your goals have to be practical before they can be achievable. Be realistic when you make your plan.

Point #4: Plan for the long term. We all hope our business will be the next Facebook—an overnight billion-dollar success story. Those kinds of businesses are few and far between. Design your business to survive the long haul by creating a one-year, three-year, five-year, seven-year, and even a ten-year plan.

Point #5: Stick to the plan. It sounds simple, but stick to the plan. You're going to have to make changes to it, but don't throw it away. When things get hard, stick to your plan.

CHAPTER 3

Work Ethic

Two Singers

I knew a young man, Max, who was an excellent singer. He sang for the president, the Queen of England, Desmond Tutu. This guy could really sing.

A friend of his by the name of Leon could sing, too. He wasn't as good as Max, but his work ethic was better. Leon stayed up until two or three o'clock in the morning learning new songs so that he could do covers of them and put them up on YouTube. Meanwhile, at two or three in the morning, Max was in bed.

Leon ended up out in California recording his first album for a major label while Max was still stuck at home in Nevada.

That didn't happen because Leon was a better singer. It happened because he was the one who got up early every morning. He was the one who went out in the streets and sold his CDs the hard way. He was the one who kept knocking on producers' doors until one of them opened up.

He was the one with the work ethic.

Work Ethic: Act on the Plan

Everybody writes a plan, and then they say, "Well, I'm going to start this next week."

I say, "No! Don't wait. Get started." Put the plan into action. Take that plan and bring it to life.

The way you bring your plan to life is by having a strong work ethic.

As an entrepreneur, you will work harder on your own business than any other business you've ever worked for in your life. You're not just walking into a company where someone else has a dream and has put that dream into action. *You* have the dream. You are planning and working the dream.

That means you are the first one there in the morning, and the last one to leave at night. You're the energy source of your business. Not just some days. Every day. After you achieve a certain level of success, this will change. Others will step up and help you drive the company. But that doesn't happen by itself. You have to build it with your own strong work ethic in the first place.

The goal is to work smarter. Do more with less. Use your work ethic to build a business that becomes a sustainable machine that only requires servicing periodically. That servicing is also known as "executive leadership," and it's where you're headed when you start the journey with a strong work ethic.

Without a strong work ethic, your business will veer off the plan, and your dream will be contaminated. Why? Because your business takes on the same work ethic that you have yourself. If you're five or ten minutes late to work, your employees will be twenty to thirty minutes late. If you take an extra ten minutes for lunch, your employees will take an extra fifteen to twenty minutes for lunch.

Remember, this is your dream. If you don't want to work hard to make it succeed, why should anybody else?

The Point Guard Entrepreneur: Work to Succeed

The point guard in basketball uses his work ethic to set the bar for his team. Everything he expects from the other players, he does himself. He's the first one in the gym, but before he gets to the gym, he's in the weight room. The other guys walk by and say, "Hey, we can't let him be stronger than us." They join him in the weight room. Then the point guard goes and shoots one hundred shots before practice. The other guys say, "Wow, he's going to work out for an hour and then he's going to shoot a hundred shots before practice? We've got to follow him."

The point guard pushes his team without having to open his mouth. He encourages them to succeed with his actions.

A point guard entrepreneur leads by example the same way. If someone walks into your office and says, "The bathroom is overflowing," you don't just sit there. You roll up your sleeves and go clean that up. If you don't do it as the owner, why should the people working for you do the same?

You drive forward movement by demonstrating forward movement yourself.

When leading by example doesn't work, that's when you call a time out. For example, you could sit the teammate who isn't following your lead down, and you could say, "You know, thank you for everything you do. I really appreciate it. But you know, I've noticed that everybody else on the team washes up the microwave, and I haven't seen you do that yet.

"Now I know that's not part of your job, but we all are working for the same dream, aren't we? We're all trying to get better. You want a raise one day, right? To get better, we have to work as a team. Because when the team wins, we all win. But you know what? You did a great job writing that proposal last week. I really appreciate it. And I want to personally thank you for that. Thanks for your time. Have a great day, all right?"

You inspire a strong work ethic in your team by acknowledging what they do well first, then explaining what you'd like them to correct. Always end those conversations on a positive note. That's how you drive work ethic as a point guard entrepreneur.

Five Points to Create a Strong Work Ethic for Success

Point #1: Create and practice a steady routine. If you go to bed at nine and wake up at five, then consistently go to bed at nine and wake up at five. A steady routine strengthens your work ethic.

Point #2: Draw energy from your team. When you feel rundown, use the energy of your team to build your work ethic back up again.

Point #3: Revisit the dream. Remind yourself why you're working so hard by revisiting your dream, your goal, or your purpose.

Point #4: Act on the plan. Don't wait. A plan without action has no value. A plan combined with a strong work ethic leads to success.

Point #5: Relax. You must find time to relax. I'm not talking about a day, and I'm not talking about five hours. I'm talking about twenty minutes of meditation. Whatever you need to get your mind away from everything so you can recoup. Eat right, and be in good health. When you take the time to restore yourself, your work ethic becomes the best that it can be.

CHAPTER 4

Willingness to Fail

On the Line

When I launched my property preservation business, I started with employees. We were doing pretty well. Then one day, one of my people said, "You know, we could make more money if we had contractors doing most of this work."

Now, understand that I'd already drawn a business plan. I'd put it into action, and I'd hired employees. I could see that my team member was right: we could make more money with contractors than employees. I also knew that if I failed, I couldn't hold up my end of the contract to my bank.

I decided that I was willing to fail.

I changed that business from employees to contractors. Did I fire everybody I had? No. I offered them the opportunity to go out into the field in their own trucks. The transition was hard. I had a lot on the line. But it paid off in the end.

In 2013, we did $780,000's worth of business through contractors. We're still growing. But to achieve that success, I had to be willing to fail.

Willing to Fail, Prepared to Succeed

Failure is a part of success. There are very few people in the world who have not failed at something before they became successful. Thomas Edison, the Wright Brothers, Walt Disney. Donald Trump went bankrupt seven times before he made his fortune.

Did all of those people experience failure? Yes, they did. But failure was just a part of their success. You have to understand that failure will happen, but that failure also comes with some of life's greatest lessons.

Some of your plans as an entrepreneur will fail. But if you're not willing to fail, if you're not willing to take chances, you may never reach success.

If you're not willing to fail, you may never get started.

Another danger of being unwilling to fail is that you may always start with plan B. Plan A looks too dangerous, so you don't even touch it. You play it safe instead, and when you play it safe you never go on the offensive. Even if you avoid crashing your ego, if you do things this way, you're never going to have the power it takes to achieve your big dreams.

Plan B is planning to fail, in my eyes. That's why a point guard entrepreneur always goes for plan A.

The Point Guard Entrepreneur: Fail to Succeed

Let's take it to the basketball court again. The point guard is driving the ball over the court with 2.5 seconds left in the game. The score is neck and neck. He has two choices: he can take the final shot himself, or he can pass the ball to another player and let that guy take the shot.

If he passes to another player, he passes the responsibility for failing off to his teammate. If takes the shot himself, he knows that everyone will blame him for losing if he misses—the same as they'll love him if he makes it.

If he takes the shot, because he's willing to take the consequences. He's willing to fail.

As a point guard entrepreneur, you need to own that same responsibility. You have to get yourself to believe that it's okay to fail. You have to understand that you will take detours that might not work in this business, but at the end of the day your willingness to fail will lead you to success.

Don't look at failure as a negative thing. Look at it as something that helps you. Your business is a journey. If you fail, at least you can say you did something, even if it didn't work. If you never do anything, that journey never starts. And that's the real failure.

That's why point guard entrepreneurs know to look at failure in a positive light.

Five Points to Succeed through Your Willingness to Fail

Point #1: Try new ideas and methods. New ideas and methods can get you to the success you want quicker. Sometimes they're the only way to achieve success. Try them without the fear of failing.

Point #2: Try new people. New people might bring in ideas that aren't familiar to you. But those ideas might have potential you haven't even dreamed about yet. Give your people the chance to be creative, even if it looks like a risk.

Point #3: Don't compare yourself to other people. It might look like others are moving faster than you are, but you don't know what's really going on within someone else's organization. Don't use the success of others as an excuse not to be willing to fail yourself.

Point #4: Dream a new dream. Sometimes your business just doesn't work out through no fault of your own. When that happens, don't give up as an entrepreneur. Go back to sleep, and dream a new dream.

Point #5: Don't give up. Understand that failure will happen. But also understand that with failure comes success. Don't give up on your dream.

CHAPTER 5

Support System

Magic Johnson's Support System

A few years ago, I had the pleasure of meeting Norm Nixon. Norm was one of the outstanding point guards for the Los Angeles Lakers between 1977 and 1983. I had his jersey in a frame, and I took it with me up on stage for him to sign. One of the things I asked him while he was signing it was, "Norm, what was the highlight of your career?"

Norm Nixon looked at me and he said, "It was grooming Magic Johnson, the next point guard."

Norm had won the NBA championships twice. He was a two-time NBA all-star. His success was enormous. But the highlight of his career was mentoring his successor, Magic Johnson.

That's the kind of support system that creates legends. And it did.

Get Support, Gain Success

What is a support system?

Your support system is the network of people keeping you sharp behind the scenes. Your friends, your family, your mentors are all part of your support system. Even the books and audio recordings of the people you look up to factor into your support system as an entrepreneur.

Your support system is the number one asset you have for your mental mindset. A strong support system is the voice that says "You're going to make it" when things get hard. It's the voice that keeps you focused on what you came here to do. A good support system is your belief network, your encouragement center, and your failsafe. When you feel like you're failing, your support system will be there to say, "Wait a minute, you worked hard for this dream. Keep going."

Without a support system in your life, success is going to be very difficult to reach. Naysayers will have a much easier time talking you out of your dreams. Even people you look on as friends will tell you that you're losing your mind. You'll hear a lot of "I told you so's." You might not even get started, because everything those naysayers say is going to make good common sense to a person who doesn't share your dream.

Your support system does share your dream. That's why it drives you to achieve success.

The Point Guard Entrepreneur: Support Your Success

The support system for a point guard in basketball is the coach and the assistant coaches. They know how the plan should work: they sat down with the point guard and developed it. When the point guard has a rough day out there on the court, what do you think his support system is telling him? Those coaches are reminding him, "Hey, the plan works. We've just got to execute it. Stay with it, don't give up on it."

Your support system does the same thing for you as a point guard entrepreneur.

There will be times when the road to achieving your dreams will be hard. That's why you have to choose your support system carefully. You might be strapped financially, and your friends want to go out for drinks on Friday night. You have to sit there and say, "Hey, I'm just going to have one drink."

If those friends are not part of your support system, they're going to give you a hard time about that. "Maybe you should get a real job," they'll say. "You were doing better than this when you were working."

But if those friends are part of your support system, they'll order one drink with you. They'll sit right by you at your table and order the spaghetti instead of the T-bone steak, and they'll be happy with a glass of wine instead of a whole bottle. Then they'll call you during the week and say, "You're doing a great job with your business. Keep it up."

They understand your struggles, and they create a positive environment to keep your motivation up and your work ethic going strong. That's why the people who surround you on a daily basis are so important.

That's why every point guard entrepreneur has a strong support system waiting in the wings.

Five Points to Use Your Support System for Success

Point #1: Refer to your support system daily. Connecting with your support system often keeps your energy up and ensures that your mindset stays on track for success.

Point #2: Read something motivational or supportive daily. Read books, articles, blogs—anything that's written by successful entrepreneurs who you look up to. Their success stories keep your inspiration and drive for personal success going strong.

Point #3: Surround yourself with mentors. Your mentors are at different stages of the journey to success. They can relate to the problems and issues you're going through, and they can help you work through them as you move forward.

Point #4: Don't be afraid to share. Share your triumphs and your failures with your support system. Don't let your ego get in the way of learning.

Point #5: Choose your support system wisely. Everybody who claims to be supporting you may not be. Choose your support system wisely, and make the hard decisions you need to make in order to achieve your dream.

CHAPTER 6

Free Throw

Wealth versus Riches

By now you may know what your definition of success is. But what is your definition of wealth?

Wealth is different from riches. Riches is defined by how much money you have. But wealth goes far beyond that.

I believe that wealth is having something that I can pass on to my kids and my grandkids. For me, wealth is not money, but the ability to make money. That's wealth. If I build a good solid foundation that brings us everything we need to live out our wildest dreams, and if I can pass that foundation on to the generations after me, that's my definition of wealth.

Wealth is freedom. It's the ability to do what you want to do, when you want to do it. A lot of entrepreneurs get obsessed with stockpiling riches. They're all about the money.

They get so caught up in riches, they forget to live.

Five Points to Thrive Beyond Your Business

A dream. A plan. A strong work ethic. A willingness to fail. And a strong support system.

These five points don't just make you successful in the business world. They are also the key plays that help you thrive in life beyond your business. When you use all five of these points, they leave you with a quality that has the ultimate ability to create balance and prosperity in your life: discipline.

It takes discipline to stick to your dream when all the odds look like they're stacked against you. It takes discipline to follow a plan from start to finish. It takes discipline to develop a steady routine and work your hardest every day. It takes discipline to be willing to fail when everything you've built is on the line. And it takes discipline to cut down on the time you spend with lifelong friends who can't see your vision, and aren't part of your support system.

But once you cultivate that discipline, life becomes one enormous window of opportunity.

If you're married and your wife says, "Honey, I've looked at our finances. And when we go on vacation, you can only play golf two days instead of four," your discipline teaches you not to see that as a limitation. Instead, you say, "She's going to cut down on expenses for the sake of our future. And I'm going to play golf two days, and love spending the other two days with her."

You have the power to turn negatives into positives. You have the power to create a well-balanced life-style that's custom-made for you.

You've become a point guard entrepreneur. And you've become the point guard of your life as well.

www.ingramcontent.com/pod-product-compliance
Lightning Source LLC
Chambersburg PA
CBHW071542170526
45166CB00004B/1518